The Surprise Box

by Francis Robin

Illustrated by Toni Goffe

Editorial Offices: Glenview, Illinois • Parsippany, New Jersey • New York, New York
Sales Offices: Needham, Massachusetts • Duluth, Georgia • Glenview, Illinois
Coppell, Texas • Sacramento, California • Mesa, Arizona

Marta loves her big sister Rosa.
Rosa calls her "Martita."
That means "little Marta."

One day, the girls are walking.
Marta finds a butterfly wing.
The butterfly wing makes her happy.
She puts it in her special box.

Rosa puts a blue ribbon in Marta's hair.
The ribbon makes Marta happy.
Marta puts the ribbon in the box.

Rosa helps Marta with her homework.
The teacher gives Marta a star.
Marta puts the star in her special box.

box

Marta loves the butterfly wing.
She loves the ribbon and the star.
She loves her big sister.
Marta thinks of a surprise for Rosa.

Marta wraps the box in colored paper.
She gives it to Rosa.
"I made you a surprise box!"
says Marta.
"You are a good big sister."

Rosa opens the box.
She sees the butterfly wing.
She sees the ribbon and the star.
"You are a good little sister," says Rosa.
"The surprise box makes me happy!"